Triple Point

Triple Point

Laura Story Johnson

Etchings Press
Indianapolis, Indiana

This publication is made possible by funding provided by the
Shaheen College of Arts and Sciences and the Department
of English at the University of Indianapolis. Special thanks
to the students who judged, edited, designed, and published
this chapbook: Abby Bailey, Olivia Cameron, Desteni Guidry,
and Liza Harris.

UNIVERSITY *of*
INDIANAPOLIS

Published by Etchings Press
1400 E. Hanna Ave.
Indianapolis, Indiana 46227
All rights reserved

etchings.uindy.edu
www.uindy.edu/cas/english

Printed by IngramSpark

Published in the United States of America

ISBN 978-1-955521-07-9

26 25 24 23 22   1 2 3 4 5

Interior Design by Abby Bailey and Liza Harris

Cover Design by Olivia Cameron

Cover Image by Diana Polekhina

Table of Contents

Acknowledgements

SKJ, for a dialogic foundation
and requisite epistemology.
B and N, for gathering stardust.
A, for sketching the recalibration.

I. Colloid

We bunked with a Mongolian man and his grand-daughter. When everything finally lurched to a stop at the border, a Chinese guard stepped into our compartment and silently pointed something metal at my forehead. It took me a few sinking moments before I realized it wasn't a gun. I only recognized her weapon as a thermometer because my dad is a large animal veterinarian. Time seemed to freeze as she aimed it at us one by one. And then, like the train we were on, rolled forward again as she moved to the next compartment, never speaking a word.

SARS stands for Severe Acute Respiratory Syndrome and was recognized by the World Health Organization four months before I left Mongolia. The warn-ing against travel to Beijing was lifted days before we arrived in the summer-heavy city. The day we bought our tickets for the train my mother called to warn us what she was hearing on the news. I told her not to worry. China's government said it wasn't that bad. We arrived on a muggy June after-noon and, starving, wandered into a corner shop. Guanz we would have said in Mongolian. I didn't know the Chinese word. I didn't know any Chinese words and so we spent our time in Beijing playing menu roulette. Point at a character that looked interesting and eat whatever came. At one guanz I watched a man slurp a pile of snails so heavy I could only think of drowning. Frantically I tried to determine which character least resembled a mollusk as he ordered another round. The first night in our youth hostel someone vomited for hours in the tiny, shared bathroom. A man's voice croaked profanities about Chinese food when he finally relented at dawn. We were all awake.

SARS was caused by a coronavirus.

A coronavirus.

A word I never could have anticipated would someday fall from the lips of my two-year-old nephew in the middle of a game. "We can't go there because of the coronavirus," he told my sister last week. SARS usually began with a high fever, hence the arming of border patrol with thermometers. Spread through close contact, droplets carrying the virus from an infected person were the most enthusiastic warriors. Sneezing and coughing could propel the virus up to six feet. Touching a contaminated surface and then the face could cause infection. Later it was determined that the virus itself may have become airborne. I was used to seeing my students in

Ulaanbaatar come to class in surgical masks when they were ill, but I wasn't prepared for the streets of Beijing to look like the floor of a hospital ward.

Infection. Contamination. Outbreak.

Disease is the original border architect.

If disease, by ignoring borders, manages to create them, what is the anti-architect? How can something be built and unbuilt at the same time?

The triple point of a substance is the single point at which all three phases can coexist in a stable equilibrium. Solid. Liquid. Gas. The triple point is a state of balance. But is balance possible? After something occurs, do we ever return to nothing? To the before? Isolated from its surroundings, a system that is in thermodynamic equilibrium will experience no changes. No net flows of matter or energy. No phase changes. No unbalanced potentials. There are no driving forces within a system when it is in thermodynamic equilibrium. In a way, the borders of existence disappear. What is the triple point of an outbreak?

Before SARS there had been an outbreak of foot and mouth disease in the countryside around Ulaan-

3

baatar. I only recognized the severity because my dad is a large animal veterinarian. A virus that causes a fever and rash in humans, foot and mouth disease decimates livestock herds because of how contagious it is, jumping between cows, sheep, goats, pigs, animals with "divided hoofs."

Cloven hooves.

A single detection of foot and mouth disease can stop international trade completely, devastating the livelihoods of nomadic herders. In a country where the production of livestock employs one out of every four Mongolians, outbreaks of foot and mouth disease can result in martial law. Returning to the city one weekend, our driver joined a long line of vehicles waiting to be sprayed down by officials in protective gear. We had travelled to visit a monastery. And yet, somehow, I had never felt so unclean. Back in my apartment, miles on foot from the nearest laundromat, I washed my clothes in the bathtub. I strung a rope across my balcony and hung everything, still dripping, to dry. Coal dust hung in the heavy winter air like vapor and painted the ice with streaks. The water in my bathtub was black by the time I finished. Soot collected on the white ceramic.

In Ulaanbaatar, my apartment windows faced west.

I watched the sun sink behind the foggy curtain of smog. In the morning, when I returned to the balcony to remove my clothing, everything was frozen. I set the jeans, t-shirts, sweatshirts around the living room like modern sculptures. Balanced, they stood on their own. I photographed the strange and vibrant equipoise. Years later the photographs, developed at a shop by the black market, have lost nearly all color. The cold petrified ghosts of the living lurch forward into the past.

They are the temperature of grey.

II. Plasma

The kelvin is how we measure the color temperature of light. The triple point of water is used to define the kelvin, which is the base unit of thermodynamic temperature. Sunset and sunrise have a color temperature of 1,850 kelvin. Mongolia is called the land of the blue sky and is the coldest place I have ever lived. Yet a clear blue poleward sky has a color temperature of between 15,000 and 27,000 kelvin – over ten times the temperature of sunrise.

The second coldest place I have ever lived is bush Alaska. Deep in the tundra the ground is so cold that it can stay frozen for years at a time, a state called permafrost. The permafrost affects ground water levels and the ability to lay pipes. Homes must be built on posts set on wooden pads that act like snowshoes, preventing them from sinking. Water tanks must be above ground, refilled by trucks at regular expensive intervals.

In Alaska, my roommate and I lived with the woman who had hired us for weeks before we were able to find our own place. Tired of sleeping on the floor, we took the first apartment that came available. It was dirty and more than we could afford, but it was ours and it was furnished. The landlord justified the price because we wouldn't have to pay to refill the water tank, shared with several other units. We signed the lease and I agreed to pay most of the rent, as my partner would eventually be joining us from the lower forty-eight and would chip in.

My roommate had to travel the first weekend in our new place and so I cleaned. Alone, I blasted Johnny Cash and strung tapestries over the holes in the wall, put new sheets on my lumpy mattress, pretended that a sputtering dust buster would take care of the ancient shag carpet's buried past. I washed and scrubbed and managed, single-handedly, to empty the entire apartment complex water tank. One of my neighbors knocked on my door to inquire if we had water. I hid the wet rag in my hand behind my back and lied. He walked away, muttering profanities about the unknown thief under his breath. From then on, I was careful. I turned the water off while I shampooed my hair. I learned a new way of doing dishes. I would stare at the vomit-colored water in a glass, wondering at its preciousness.

Foot and mouth disease does not often kill its divided hoof host, but the pain and discomfort from the vesicles and erosions it creates lead to other symptoms.

Depression.

Loss of appetite.

Reluctance to move or stand.

These were mine as the permafrost shifted, warping the asphalt, cracking walls, sinking buildings. The water colored my hair orange. I broke up with my partner and he moved out. I had to borrow money to cover the rent. The tundra died. I had a job but no work. My ex got drunk and tried to break down my door. Every morning I lingered in the break room taking as long as I could to pour a mug of bad cof fee before resigning myself to a lonely desk with no purpose. Isolated from my surroundings, there were too many driving forces.

My ability to believe eroded.

A stationary point in the orbit of a planet is a point where the motion of the planet seems to stop before restarting in the other direction. This occurs because the planet reaches a critical point. Do we have to pass through critical points to reach a state of balance?

Is erosion necessary to uncover the foundation from which we can pivot?

III. Amorphous

I had been in Africa no more than thirty minutes when an American woman like myself started talking to me about God. She was sitting in the sticky air of the Johannesburg airport, her hands neatly folded across her lap. As I watched the young woman practice her proselytizing, I envied her ability to believe. She was comforted, tying herself to a stranger. I, on the other hand, suffered the unease with which my disengaged answers resonated. I felt disconnected from everyone. It was not simply my role as the nonpartisan researcher, it was deeper. It stemmed from the conversations I had started prior to my departure. Conversations about love. Conversations that had forced me to examine what I really meant when I tried to ward off real believers by saying I was a member of their faith. I was lying, just like they did to customs officers in countries where evangelizing was prohibited, where they proclaimed to be tourists.

It was easier for me to play the part and rustle up memories of church as a child than it was to confront the truth. I even hoped by saying it maybe I'd finally settle in devotion. My practice was cultural relativism, but it left me feeling empty. I had always thought of myself as spiritual, but where my breath met my heart felt hollow. I wanted to gulp in the air of meaning, for connection to pull my soul back into that space. And so, I listened intently when the woman at my guesthouse shared her story of redemption.

Her story was whispered. She had been unable to walk, and doctors had no explanation. This form of witchcraft has plagued Christian missionaries to Africa for centuries. After months of lying paralyzed in a hospital bed, one day a nurse asked her to state her faith in God. Her proclamation saved her because she believed. Early in the morning, as I loaded my bag into the back of the truck that was to take me on a three-day drive to my next destination, I looked at the twisting branches of the trees above and feared their memory of my own faithless assertions.

They left Angola because of the war. The war for independence became a war between countrymen, decades that drove over a million people away. I went there to conduct interviews with them. I asked questions and looked into eyes that had witnessed horrors I couldn't comprehend. Alone in my room in a gated compound at night, I listened into the unremitting quiet. When the storm is so massive, the silence that follows is uneasy. I tried to understand falling asleep with the fear of eternal remembrance behind closed eyes. I tried to imagine lying on the bare ground, soul taut, stomach tense. Aid packages handed out with the name of my country on them could not feed that kind of hunger.

I tried to recall passages, words that could ease suffering, but my head was filled with Portuguese. I didn't know how to pray in Portuguese. I used a match to light the long, green coil that would burn all night to keep away mosquitoes and watched the thick smoke sway in the corner of my room.

It burned without a flame.

IV. Glassy

As a child I feared certain questions. How far back does time go? How big is the universe? In the dark of my bedroom, I would imagine space beyond space beyond space until I ran from infinity to my mother's arms.

Scientists are told to hang the number one hundred and thirty-seven on their walls to remind them of the unknown. One hundred and thirty-seven is considered to be the most important number in physics. One hundred and thirty-seven is the denominator of how we measure the strength with which matter couples to light. In other words, the probability that an atom will decay in a certain amount of time.

One hundred and thirty-seven determines how stars burn.

One hundred and thirty-seven determines if atoms exist at all.

When my friend found out that she was pregnant, she also learned that there was a lump on her ovary. The doctors said they could remove the growth, but they'd have to terminate the pregnancy. One mass of atoms for another. She chose unknown love and let the baby and the tumor grow. She chose faith. I whispered that I would have chosen differently. I imagined that my hunt for answers in the dark void of unknown critical points would have taken a different path.

When I met my friend's child, their skin was saran wrap. A clear plastic barrier was all that separated me from their heart. It was called the Norwood procedure, the first of three surgeries to save their life. I stared into the place where their breath met their heart. Every furious pump visible, I choked on the memory of my own words, felt this baby know the truth.

In the end, it wasn't my view through the invisible barrier that gave me goosebumps. It was the infinity of their eyes. My friend's child, their age still counted by hours, opened the vault just momentarily to look at me.

That black magic gaze was existence.

I yearned to prove their future. The doctors said the heart condition wasn't related to the tumor. It was just a matter of chance. I don't understand the theory of relativity, but I think its crux lies in the number one hundred and thirty-seven.

The number three.

The triple point.

I wrap my arms around my daughter and I fear the answers. I watch her sleep next to her brother and lie awake unable to comprehend the passage of time. There is a form of ice that takes 10,000 years to be born. In the universe this is a nanosecond. I tick off another day in my calendar and wonder how I can prove the future. Day after day vanishes into the white unknown. In mathematics, an orbit that gets longer and longer while at the same time virtually vanishing in space is known as a blue sky catastrophe.

Mongolia is the land of the blue sky.

Mongolia is the land without borders.

The blue sky catastrophe is used to model cardiac rhythms. In other words, to map the human heart. But can we create a map without borders?

Yesterday I received a video from my friend's child, who is now thirteen. Their black magic gaze still takes my breath and I feel it meet my heart. I feel my soul pulled into that space. My children exist and I am vulnerable. Our children exist and we are all vulnerable. Maybe I don't fear the questions. Maybe I fear the answers because attaining them requires sacrifice.

Maybe without division, we can't exist.

Maybe without division, we can't love.

V. Crystalline

When we came upon her body in the road, the bowl she had been carrying was just beyond her fingertips. The grains she had filled it with were spilled into the shadows, covered in ugly sand. I was sitting in the back of the vehicle with two women we had picked up along the way. Our driver stopped and his wife, a nurse, got out. I could see the young girl's body, a silhouette in the meager headlight. I thought she was dead. The nurse carried her back to us, asked the women if they knew her. She had foam oozing between her lips and her eyes were fluttering, gently.

Quietly, so quietly, the women told us where to take her. She had no mother. This wasn't the first time she had been stranded by her own body in the darkness.

The darkness followed us to her extended family. A half-dozen half-clad children gathered. They were excited by the appearance of a vehicle and paid no attention to the reappearance of the missing girl. Some of her cousins stepped over her, an invisible spirit in the dirt where we laid her next to their home. We explained, returned the bowl of ruined pellets. Perhaps something could be salvaged.

A toddler ran around in a sparkly pink tutu. I marveled at the reach of donation boxes and swallowed hard past the lump in my throat. We drove away.

She survived. And her survival was connected to my own. As I lay myself down that night on a mattress on the floor of the nurse's home, a half-dozen cats surrounded me. Unable to sleep, I went to the porch, scattering cats and shining a flashlight at my feet to move any potential snakes. There, in the cold of summer's winter, I stood and looked at the brilliant stars overhead.

I had gazed into that particular kind of night sky, which only exists when we are isolated from our surroundings, on a few other occasions in my life. I remembered each time as though I was still there. Each time a different form of falling in love.

Cozy in a sleeping bag at my grandparent's property.

Frightened in a remote New Mexico campsite during the off season.

Shivering outside of a radio station in bush Alaska.

Laughing at a monastery outside of Ulaanbaatar.

Joyous at a ski resort at night, alone at the top of a mountain, having finally learned to pivot.

Skiing is most effective when the temperature is near zero degrees Celsius, which is roughly the temperature of the triple point of water. A book on skiing at the triple point notes another definition: when increased understanding of the how and increased understanding of the why co-exist with an experience of awe. We use one hundred and thirty-seven to understand the how and why of the universe, but at the same time one hundred and thirty-seven reminds us that we cannot map borders onto infinity. Reminds us that our foundation is awe. Reminds us that the universe is the anti-architect. To see the galaxy, to truly see it, is faith.

Stars burn without a flame. What we perceive as fire is actually fusion. The opposite of division. The very fact that we can see stars implies a sort of universal thermodynamic equilibrium. A state of balance. Proof that we are living both the something and the nothing at the same time. Proof of the future. The farthest star we have mapped in the sky is 13.4 billion light-years from earth. This means that every time we look at it, we are seeing it as it was 13.4 billion years ago. At this very moment, the before and the after co-exist.

Without fusion, we can't exist.

Without fusion, we can't love.

On that porch along the Zambezi River, thousands of miles from every person who knew that I existed, everything lurched to a stop. Isolated from my surroundings, there was only silence. Time seemed to freeze as I stared at the stars one by one. And then, without explanation, rolled forward again as I stepped barefoot off the porch into the cool sand, never speaking a word.

Colophon

Interior text is set in Merriweather. The cover fonts are from the Minion Variable Concept family.

About Etchings Press

Etchings Press is a student-run publisher at the University of Indianapolis that runs a post-publication award—the Whirling Prize—as well as an annual publication contest for one poetry chapbook, one prose chapbook, and one novella. On occasion, Etchings Press publishes new chapbooks from previous winners. For more information about these contests and the Whirling Prize post-publication award, please visit etchings.uindy.edu.

Previous winners and publications:

Poetry
2022: *A Place That Knows You* by Tiwaladeoluwa Adekunle
2022: *The Vaudeville Horse* by Elizabeth Kerlikowske
2021: *My Mother's Ghost Scrubs the Floor at 2 a.m.*
    by Robert Okaji
2020: *Vaginas Need Air* by Tori Grant Welhouse
2019: *As Lovers Always Do* by Marne Wilson
2018: *In the Herald of Improbable Misfortunes*
    by Robert Campbell
2017: *Uncle Harold's Maxwell House Haggadah*
    by Danny Caine
2016: *Some Animals* by Kelli Allen
2015: *Velocity of Slugs* by Joey Connelly
2014: *Action at a Distance* by Christopher Petruccelli

Prose

2022: *Triple Point* by Laura Story Johnson (essays)

2021: *Bad Man Love Stories* by Curtis VanDonkelaar (fiction)

2020: *Three in the Morning and You Don't Smoke Anymore* by Peter J. Stavros (fiction)

2019: *Dissenting Opinion from the Committee for the Beatitudes* by Marc J. Sheehan (fiction)

2018: *The Forsaken* by Chad V. Broughman (fiction)

2017: *Unravelings* by Sarah Cheshire (memoir)

2016: *Pathetic* by Shannon McLeod (essays)

2015: *Ologies* by Chelsea Biondolillo (essays)

2014: *Static: Stories* by Frederick Pelzer (fiction)

Novella

2022: *Goodbye to the Ocean* by Susan L. Lin

2021: *Miss Alma May Learns to Fight* by Stuart Rose

2020: *Under Black Leaves* by Doug Ramspeck

2019: *Savonne, Not Vonny* by Robin Lee Lovelace

2018: *Edge of the Known Bus Line* by James R. Gapinski

2017: *The Denialist's Almanac of American Plague and Pestilence* by Christopher Mohar

2016: *Followers* by Adam Fleming Petty

Chapbooks from Previous Winners

2022: *slighted.* by Chad V. Broughman (fiction)

2020: *Fruit Rot* by James R. Gapinski (fiction)

2016: *#LOVESONG* by Chelsea Biondolillo (microessays with photos and found text)

Laura Story Johnson is a researcher, writer, and photographer. Her creative nonfiction has appeared in literary journals and magazines, including *South Loop Review*, *Written River*, *Great Lakes Review*, *North-wind*, and *Minerva Rising*. She currently lives in Iowa with her family.

Find her online at www.laurastoryjohnson.com.

www.ingramcontent.com/pod-product-compliance
Lightning Source LLC
Chambersburg PA
CBHW070032030426
42335CB00017B/2402